The Well-Being Coaching Workbook

Jeffrey Ethan Auerbach

The Well-Being Coaching Workbook
Jeffrey Ethan Auerbach

Library of Congress Cataloging-in-Publication Data
Auerbach, Jeffrey Ethan.
The Well-Being Coaching Workbook/ Jeffrey Ethan Auerbach.—1st ed.
p. cm.

ISBN 978-0-9706834-2-7

1. Self-actualization (Psychology) 2. Mentoring 3. Executives—Training of. 4.
Leadership—study and teaching. I. Auerbach, Jeffrey.

First edition 2014

Author's note: The names and details of the coaching examples provided in this book have been changed when necessary
to respect the confidentiality of the coaching relationships.
This book is written for educational purposes only and is not intended for use as any type of psychotherapy, diagnostic
instrument or legal advice.

Printed in the United States of America.

Executive College Press
897 Oak Park Blvd. #271
Pismo Beach, CA 93449 USA
www.executivecoachcollege.com

TABLE OF CONTENTS:

WELL-BEING COACHING WORKBOOK

Introduction to Well-Being Coaching...................1

Are you Ready to be Coached?...........................2

Rapid Rise in Research 3

Goal Attainment and Quality of Life..................4

Coaching Agreement 5

Goals Guide 7

My Body-Reflections and Ideal Self.................8

Self-Assessment.. 10

Well-Being Questionnaire................................13

Well-Being Satisfaction Scale 17

Values List Exercise 20

Personal Well-Being Vision 21

Goal Design 23

My Personality Type 25

My Strengths 27

GOOD™ Model of Coaching 28

My Action Coaching Plan................................29

Options Brainstorming Worksheet................... 30

Thinking Errors 31

My Constructive Thinking Plan 32

Obstacle Busting Worksheet..........................33

Self-Management Tuning 35

Coaching Learning Journal 36

Well-Being Coaching Workbook

Introduction to Well-Being Coaching

Congratulations! Welcome to well-being coaching. You have taken an important step by hiring a well-being coach and obtaining your Well-Being Coaching Workbook. This workbook will complement what your coach has shared with you and will provide coaching forms and tools that will be critical to your coaching success.

What is coaching?

Coaching is a specialized helping relationship with a trained coach, who helps you move forward with your most important well-being goals. A coach is a thought-partner who will help you clarify your goals, build motivation, assist you in designing action steps, and discuss how to manage any obstacles that might hinder your success.

Your coach will:

- Help you clarify your most important goals
- Introduce tools available to you
- Help you move forward more quickly

Provide support and encouragement and honest feedback.

The coaching philosophy comes with two essential beliefs: that you are the expert on your own life, and that you are creative and resourceful. Hence, your coach will ask you lots of questions. Through the art of the coaching conversation, it is you who will most of the time be able to arrive at the ideas and solutions that will be most helpful to you.

A few words about what coaching is not. Well-being coaching is not mental health counseling. Coaching is also not consulting. A consultant would give you expert advice, perhaps even do (some of) the work for you. Although your coach may be an expert in areas of interest to you—such as stress-management or exercise and fitness—the coach's primary role is not to give you expert advice. Although sometimes a coach will, selectively, offer advice, the coach's main objective is to help you strategize to find your unique way, the one that works best for you in manifesting your ideal state.

The coaching process will usually consist of regularly scheduled meetings, which may be conducted via telephone, videoconference, or in person, and you will be expected to do homework, such as following through on your action steps. Your coach's strategy will likely draw as much as possible from you, to help you mine your creativity and resources. This approach, with you owning your action steps, will result in greater success than if someone else tells you what to do. So when the coach does assign homework or offer specific advice, you are free to do the assignment or not, to take the advice or not. Now, if advice your coach has given doesn't feel like a good match for you, you will be encouraged to share your thinking, perhaps even come up with a "counter-offer." This style of professional guidance involves you taking responsibility for moving forward—with the support of your coach.

Some coaches like to create agreements at the outset about some details of the coaching process. For example, requesting permission in advance to challenge you if it seems you're not stretching as much as you could, or, should your conversation go astray, to occasionally guide you back to your exploration dialogue and planning. But know that such requests are done in the name of supporting you in getting into action.

Your coach will also have you complete a coaching agreement detailing information such as the frequency of sessions, fee, duration of the coaching engagement, and how confidentiality will be handled, for example.

Are you Ready to be Coached?

Here is a short questionnaire for you to complete to assess your readiness for coaching:

Name: _____

This questionnaire is designed to help you self-assess your readiness for a coaching relationship. Please mark Yes or No to each question:

1. I will keep appointments with myself to work on my coaching homework.
    ☐ Yes   ☐ No

2. There is something I want to work on or achieve which I will focus on in my coaching.
    ☐ Yes   ☐ No

3. I am willing to stop or change behaviors that are interfering with my progress.
    ☐ Yes   ☐ No

4. I am willing to try new approaches to help me achieve my goals.
    ☐ Yes   ☐ No

5. Coaching is an appropriate approach to help me accomplish my goals, as opposed to therapy for an emotional issue, consulting for specific problem solving, or specific teaching.
    ☐ Yes   ☐ No

6. I will take regular actions to help achieve my coaching goals even if I don't see immediate results.
    ☐ Yes   ☐ No

7. I will be open with my coach about what I like or don't like about how the coaching is going.
    ☐ Yes   ☐ No

8. I will work collaboratively with my coach to design goals and action steps to move forward.
    ☐ Yes   ☐ No

Coaching Works

Though coaching is a relatively new field, an estimated 50,000 professional coaches are now in practice. And as the popularity of coaching has grown, the amount of research being conducted on coaching effectiveness has also skyrocketed—as you can see in the "Rapid Rise in Coaching Research" chart. Two other diagrams depict findings on the effectiveness of coaching, indicating both goal attainment and quality of life before and after well-being coaching. As you can see, the research shows that after coaching, many people have made significant progress on their goals, and their well-being significantly improved.

RAPID RISE IN COACHING RESEARCH

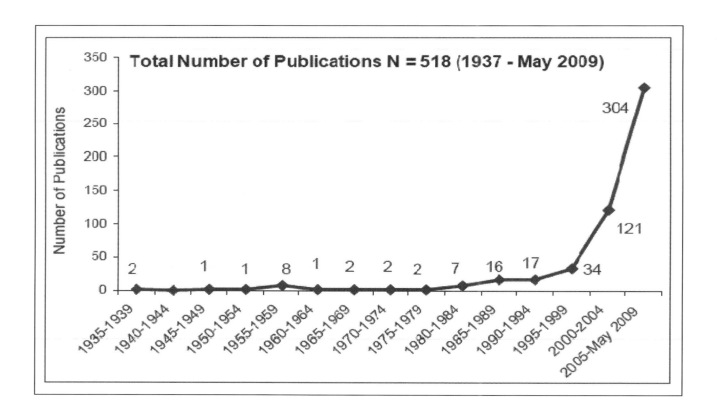

GOAL ATTAINMENT, PRE AND POST

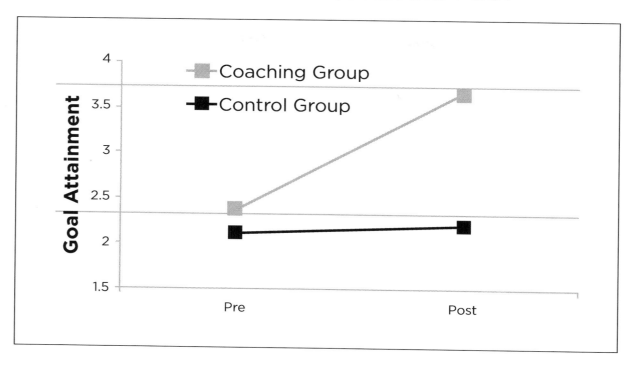

QUALITY OF LIFE, PRE AND POST

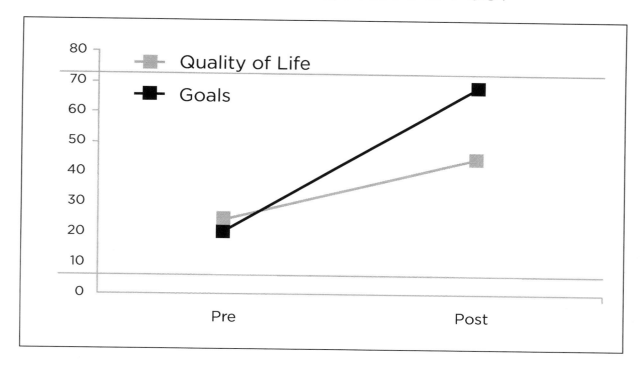

WELL-BEING COACHING AGREEMENT

To my client: please review, adjust, sign where indicated, and return to me. Thank you.

Name_____

Initial term_____months, from _____ through _____

Fee $_____ per month, $_____ for the ____ month project

Session day _____Session time _____

Number of sessions per month_____ Duration_____(length of scheduled session)

Referred by: _____

COACHING STRUCTURE:
- Client calls the coach at the scheduled time.
- Client pays coaching fees in advance.
- Client pays for long-distance charges, if any.

1. As a client, I understand and agree that I am responsible for my physical, mental and emotional well-being during my coaching calls, including my choices and decisions. I am aware that I can choose to discontinue coaching at any time.

2. I understand that "coaching" is a professional-client relationship I have with my coach which is designed to facilitate the creation/development of personal or professional goals, and to develop and carry out a plan to help achieve those goals.

3. I understand that coaching is a comprehensive process that may involve many areas of my life, including work, finances, health, relationships, education and recreation. I acknowledge that deciding how to handle these issues, incorporate coaching into those areas, and implement my choices is exclusively my responsibility.

4. I understand that coaching does not involve the diagnosis or treatment of mental disorders. I understand that coaching is not a substitute for counseling or mental health care or substance abuse treatment and I will not use it in place of diagnosis, treatment or therapy.

5. I agree that if I am currently in therapy or otherwise under the care of a mental health professional, I have consulted with the mental health care provider regarding the advisability of working with a coach, and the provider is aware of my decision to proceed with the coaching relationship.

continued on next page

6. I understand that information will generally be held as confidential unless I state otherwise, in writing, except as required by law or for other ethical reasons.

7. I understand that certain topics may be anonymously and hypothetically shared with other coaching professionals for training or consultation purposes.

8. I understand that coaching is not to be used as a substitute for professional advice by legal, medical, financial, business, spiritual or other qualified professionals. I will seek independent professional guidance for legal, medical, mental health treatment, financial, business, spiritual or other matters. I understand all decisions in these areas are exclusively mine and I acknowledge my decisions and my actions regarding them are my sole responsibility.

I have read and agree to the above.

Client Signature:_____ Date: _____

GOALS GUIDE

Here is a list of popular goals that you may want to work toward with your coach. Please put a check mark next to the goals you are most interested in achieving.

HEALTH AND EMOTIONAL WELL-BEING

- ☐ Have more fun
- ☐ Reduce sugar/fat intake
- ☐ Sleep better
- ☐ Increase optimism
- ☐ Exercise more
- ☐ Reduce alcohol/nicotine intake
- ☐ Begin a spiritual practice
- ☐ Reduce stress
- ☐ Lose weight

CAREER

- ☐ Undergo job training
- ☐ Design a career track
- ☐ Reduce stress on the job
- ☐ Rejuvenate career
- ☐ Get a raise or promotion
- ☐ Start own business
- ☐ Get a better job
- ☐ Be more productive at work

FINANCIAL

- ☐ Invest more regularly
- ☐ Buy a home
- ☐ Set up and follow a budget
- ☐ Obtain needed insurance
- ☐ Earn more money
- ☐ Build financial reserve
- ☐ Save more
- ☐ Face a money challenge
- ☐ Create lifetime money plan
- ☐ Plan pre- or postretirement finances
- ☐ Reduce debts or credit cards
- ☐ Curtail overspending
- ☐ Design financial independence plan

RELATIONSHIPS

- ☐ Socialize more
- ☐ Get closer to family
- ☐ Get closer to spouse
- ☐ Create a satisfying personal relationship

TRANSITION

- ☐ New job
- ☐ Medical challenge
- ☐ Loss of loved one
- ☐ Retirement planning
- ☐ Move beyond trauma
- ☐ Major financial change
- ☐ Recover from a divorce

OTHER

- ☐ Live more congruently with core values
- ☐ Complete special project
- ☐ Practice patience
- ☐ Lead a more spiritual life
- ☐ Begin recovery
- ☐ Express more gratitude
- ☐ Create a new life vision
- ☐ Take more responsibility
- ☐ Express creativity
- ☐ Become more disciplined
- ☐ Find a mentor
- ☐ Participate in mediation

MY BODY - MY REFLECTIONS

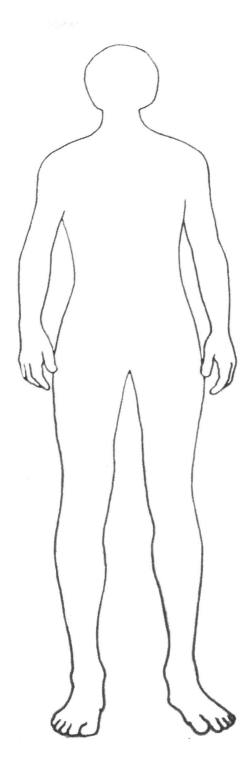

Use this outline to document how you see your body right now. Include how you feel about your whole body - inside and out. Make any notes you would like to on the page.

MY BODY - MY IDEAL SELF

Use this outline to imagine your ideal self. Make notes in and around the form about how you would like it to be. Compare the two diagrams and think about how you see yourself. What you have written will give you clues. Ask yourself the following questions:

1. **What do I see as positive about myself?**

2. **Are there more positives or negatives noted?**

3. **Could I have written more positives about myself?**

If so add them here:

4. **Which of the negative notes are changeable? Which do I need to accept?**

5. **What is important about making each change?**

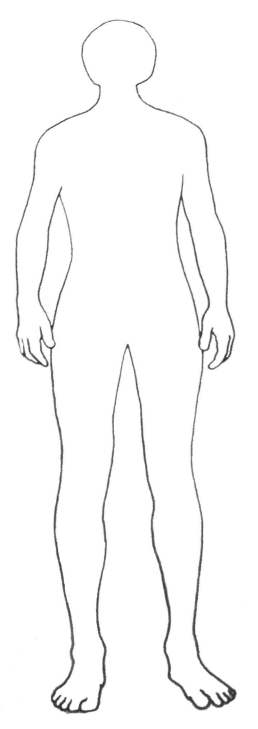

PERSONAL COACHING SELF-ASSESSMENT

Name_____ Date_____

Directions: Place a check mark next to the statements accurate for you now. If you feel a statement does not relate to you put N/A. The statements left blank may indicate areas draining your energy and that you may want to focus on in coaching.

RELATIONSHIPS

_____ I enjoy the company of my special friends.

_____ I share my life with a special person.

_____ I have a blood family or a chosen family that loves and supports me.

_____ I get immediate pleasure from spending time with children.

_____ I have a pet that brings me joy and provides me with unconditional love.

_____ I spend time having fun with people who make me laugh.

_____ I am part of a loving and supportive community.

_____ I have told my parents, in the past three months, that I love them.

_____ I get along well with my sibling(s).

_____ I do not gossip or talk about others.

_____ I receive enough love from people around me to feel good.

_____ I quickly correct miscommunications and misunderstandings when they do occur.

_____ I am at peace with past lovers or spouses.

_____ I do not judge or criticize others.

_____ I have a best friend or a soul mate.

_____ I spend time with people who don't try to change me.

ENVIRONMENT

_____ I have a special "soul nurturing" place in my home just for me.

_____ I listen to my favorite music regularly.

_____ I love my sense of style and feel good in the clothes I wear.

_____ I've let go of all the "stuff" I no longer need.

___ I keep fresh flowers in my home and office.

___ My home is neat, clean, and well organized.

___ I create beauty all around me.

___ I live in a home/apartment I love.

___ People feel comfortable in my home.

___ I live in the geographical area of my choice.

___ I am not damaged by my environment.

___ I recycle.

BODY, MIND, AND SPIRIT

___ I exercise regularly.

___ I have eliminated caffeine from my diet.

___ I have a way to relax that eliminates stress and keeps me feeling centered.

___ I eat healthy and nutritious foods.

___ Each day I read something inspirational to keep my attitude positive.

___ I set aside regular time for solitude and silence.

___ I have a spiritual practice that connects me with my Wise Self.

___ My hair is the way I want it.

___ My cholesterol count is healthful.

___ My blood pressure is healthful.

___ I do not smoke tobacco or other substances.

___ I do not use illegal drugs or misuse prescribed medications.

___ I have had a complete eye exam within the past two years.

___ My weight is within my ideal range.

___ I walk or exercise at least three times per week.

___ I have a rewarding life beyond my work or profession.

___ I have something to look forward to every day.

___ I have no habits I find unacceptable.

WORK

____ My commute is stress free.

____ I have a mentor who guides and encourages me.

____ I always take lunch breaks.

____ I have colleagues who inspire and respect me.

____ I take mental health days when I need them.

____ I enjoy my work.

____ I feel energized at the end of most workdays.

____ I am consistently early or easily on time.

____ I consistently take evenings, weekends, and holidays off and take at least two weeks vacation each year.

MONEY

____ I always carry enough cash with me.

____ I am fully insured and protected.

____ I save money consistently.

____ My taxes are paid and up to date.

____ I've made smart investments that earn me top dollar.

____ I enjoy being generous and easily share my wealth.

____ I pay my credit cards in full each month.

____ I pay my bills on time, virtually always.

____ I know how much I must have to be minimally financially independent, and I have a plan to get there.

____ I have six months' living expenses in a money market-type account.

____ I have excellent medical insurance.

____ I have a financial plan for the next year.

____ My will is up to date and accurate.

____ I know my financial net-worth.

____ My services are so exceptional, people gladly pay me premium rates.

AUERBACH WELL-BEING COACHING CLIENT QUESTIONNAIRE

Please take a reasonable amount of time (you define that!) to answer the following questions. There are no wrong answers. Some of the questions capture information about where you are today. Other questions will make you curious about what you want from coaching, from your career and from your life in general. I ask some general and personal questions as a way of creating a more complete understanding of you. You are free to answer the questions as briefly or as in-depth as you wish. Your answers are generally confidential, similar to our coaching conversations, unless a rare situation arises where they warrant a release of information as required by law or ethical standards, such as a danger to self or others. Your responses will help us set a strong foundation for the coaching relationship.

Name: _____

Mailing Address: _____

Home Telephone:_____ Work Telephone: _____

Mobile Telephone:_____ Fax Number: _____

E-Mail Address:_____

Occupation/Job Title and Organization Name:_____

COACHING:

1. What do you want to be sure to get from the coaching relationship? _____

_____

_____

2. How do you want me to be as your coach?_____

_____

_____

3. What do you want to work on in coaching?_____

_____

_____

4. What two steps could you take immediately to help you move forward? _____

_____

_____

5. What can I say to you when you are stuck to help you move forward? _____

_____

_____

6. What changes might you need to make to help your coaching be successful?_____

_____

_____

Career:

1. What is most positive about your career? _____

_____

2. What changes do you want to make related to career? _____

_____

3. What are your key career goals? _____

_____

4. What do you need to change to help your career move forward? _____

_____

Social Well-being: having strong and positive relationships

5. What is most positive about your relationships and social life? _____

_____

6. What changes do you want to make related to your relationships and social life? _____

_____

7. What are your key goals related to your relationships and social life? _____

_____

8. What do you need to change to help your relationships and social life move forward? _____

_____

_____

Financial Well-being: maintaining sufficient, balanced finances

9. What is most positive about your financial situation?_____

_____

10. What changes do you want to make related to your financial situation? _____

_____

11. What are your key goals related to your financial situation?_____

_____

12. What do you need to change to help your financial situation move forward? _____

_____

_____

Community Well-being: feeling engaged in one's community

13. What is most positive about your community situation? _____

_____

14. What changes do you want to make related to your community situation? _____

_____

15. What are your key goals related to your community situation? _____

_____

16. What do you need to change to help your community situation move forward? _____

_____

Physical and Psychological Well-being: living a healthy life
Please share any concerns or information you want to about:

Energy level: _____

Stress: _____

Depression/Anxiety: _____

Life Satisfaction: _____

Life Balance: _____

Exercise: _____

Weight: _____

Illness Issues: _____

Recovery Issues: _____

1. What is most positive about your health situation? _____

_____

2. What concerns do you have about your health? _____

_____

3. What changes do you want to make related to your health situation? _____
   _____

4. What are your key goals related to your health situation? _____
   _____

5. What do you need to change to help your health or a more healthy lifestyle move forward? ___
   _____
   _____
   _____

Personal

1. What special interests do you have? _____
   _____

2. What special knowledge do you have? _____
   _____

3. What do you believe in strongly? _____
   _____

4. Tell me about a time when you were operating in a peak performance phase, when things
   were going really well or you were very pleased with what you were doing or accomplishing.
   Don't be humble please. What was going on? Who was involved? What feelings did you
   have? _____
   _____
   _____
   _____
   _____
   _____
   _____

5. What do you do when things get stressful? _____
   _____

6. What activities have special meaning for you? _____
   _____

7. What vision do you have for your life? _____
   _____

8. Please tell me what you would like to about your family and personal life: _____
   _____

9. Please tell me about significant events in your life that you would like to share: _____
   _____

Auerbach Well-Being Satisfaction Scale™ 1.0

Name_____ Male_____ Female_____ Age_____

Directions: Please answer each question. For the upper choice, row A, choose a number that represents how satisfied you are in that area (overall in the past week). Then for the lower choice, choose your target satisfaction level, which is a blend of your true goal for this area factored together with how motivated you are to make changes in this area. These areas can become part of your well-being vision and your coaching agenda. What satisfaction number are you at now? What is your target satisfaction level? You may have target satisfaction scores that are the same, or different, from your current level of satisfaction. There are not necessarily right, or wrong, answers, this is entirely your choice -- you decide what is important to you.

Keep in mind that some areas may not be that important to you right now. For example, let's say you are not interested in "exercise" in this chapter of your life. You might rank this area as a "6" because you are quite satisfied with this area of your life now (although someone observing your exercise habits might rate you as lower). You are rating your satisfaction level, not other people's opinions. Let's say you are very interested in "positive relationships" in this phase of your life. You might choose to rank this a "5" if you feel generally satisfied with that area of your life. Upon reflection though, you may conclude that you feel particularly motivated to increase your "positive relationships" from a "5" to a "7", so you enter a "5" in the upper row and a "7" in the lower row.

Ranking System: 1 represents the lowest level of satisfaction and 7 represents the highest possible satisfaction.

1. Happiness
My happiness level now

A	1	2	3	4	5	6	7

Target satisfaction level

B	1	2	3	4	5	6	7

2. Engagement and Interest
The amount of engagement and interest I experience now

A	1	2	3	4	5	6	7

Target satisfaction level

B	1	2	3	4	5	6	7

3. Meaning and Purpose
The amount of meaning and purpose in my life now

A	1	2	3	4	5	6	7

Target satisfaction level

B	1	2	3	4	5	6	7

4. Positive Feelings
The level of positive feelings I feel about myself now

A	1	2	3	4	5	6	7

Target satisfaction level

B	1	2	3	4	5	6	7

5. Optimism
My optimism level now

A	1	2	3	4	5	6	7

My target optimism level

B	1	2	3	4	5	6	7

6. Relationships
The quality of my relationships with others now

A	1	2	3	4	5	6	7

Target satisfaction level

B	1	2	3	4	5	6	7

7. Friend or Partner

My feeling of closeness with a special friend or partner now

A | 1 | 2 | 3 | 4 | 5 | 6 | 7 |

Target satisfaction level

B | 1 | 2 | 3 | 4 | 5 | 6 | 7 |

8. Eating Habits

My eating habits now

A | 1 | 2 | 3 | 4 | 5 | 6 | 7 |

Target satisfaction level

B | 1 | 2 | 3 | 4 | 5 | 6 | 7 |

9. Weight

My weight now

A | 1 | 2 | 3 | 4 | 5 | 6 | 7 |

Target satisfaction level

B | 1 | 2 | 3 | 4 | 5 | 6 | 7 |

10. Exercise

My exercise behavior now

A | 1 | 2 | 3 | 4 | 5 | 6 | 7 |

Target satisfaction level

B | 1 | 2 | 3 | 4 | 5 | 6 | 7 |

11. Physical Health

My overall physical health now

A | 1 | 2 | 3 | 4 | 5 | 6 | 7 |

Target satisfaction level

B | 1 | 2 | 3 | 4 | 5 | 6 | 7 |

12. Sleep

My sleep patterns now

A | 1 | 2 | 3 | 4 | 5 | 6 | 7 |

Target satisfaction level

B | 1 | 2 | 3 | 4 | 5 | 6 | 7 |

13. Time Management

My time management now

A | 1 | 2 | 3 | 4 | 5 | 6 | 7 |

Target satisfaction level

B | 1 | 2 | 3 | 4 | 5 | 6 | 7 |

14. Stress Management

My stress level now

A | 1 | 2 | 3 | 4 | 5 | 6 | 7 |

Target satisfaction level

B | 1 | 2 | 3 | 4 | 5 | 6 | 7 |

15. Home

My home environment now

A | 1 | 2 | 3 | 4 | 5 | 6 | 7 |

Target satisfaction level

B | 1 | 2 | 3 | 4 | 5 | 6 | 7 |

16. Inner Peace

My feeling of inner peace now

A | 1 | 2 | 3 | 4 | 5 | 6 | 7 |

Target satisfaction level

B | 1 | 2 | 3 | 4 | 5 | 6 | 7 |

17. Family

My feeling of closeness to a family member (by blood or choice)

A | 1 | 2 | 3 | 4 | 5 | 6 | 7 |

Target satisfaction level

B | 1 | 2 | 3 | 4 | 5 | 6 | 7 |

18. Gratitude

My feeling of gratitude now

A | 1 | 2 | 3 | 4 | 5 | 6 | 7 |

Target satisfaction level

B | 1 | 2 | 3 | 4 | 5 | 6 | 7 |

19. Career

My career satisfaction now

Target satisfaction level

20. Financial

My financial well-being now

Target satisfaction level

B | 1 | 2 | 3 | 4 | 5 | 6 | 7

After you have completed the Well-being Satisfaction Scale, your coach and you may discuss specific goals for your coaching work. This will become the backbone of your coaching agenda. It's important that you choose your own goals – as coaches we believe that you are in the driver's seat and you will be most motivated to accomplish goals you have freely chosen yourself.

A next step your coach may do is to have you create a "Personal Well-Being Vision" statement.

VALUES LIST EXERCISE

Clarifying your values for this stage of your life can aide you in shaping your purpose and vision. In this stage of life or transition what values are most important to you? What are the values you must honor to be true to this chapter of your life?

Choose the 10 – 15 values you feel are most important at this time and group them together in strings.

Next, please identify the 3 values that feel are most important to you in this phase of your life/or in your emerging phase of life. These would be values that would be a great loss for you to not have in your life.

Example: Collaboration/Community/Full self-expression

☐ Achievement	☐ Free time	☐ Performance
☐ Accuracy	☐ Focus	☐ Personal power
☐ Acknowledgment	☐ Forward the action	☐ Peace
☐ Advancement	☐ Freedom	☐ Pleasure
☐ Adventure	☐ Friendship	☐ Productivity
☐ Aesthetics	☐ Growth	☐ Power
☐ Affection	☐ Integrity	☐ Precision
☐ Authenticity	☐ Independence	☐ Recognition
☐ Autonomy	☐ Intellectual status	☐ Responsibility
☐ Beauty	☐ Health	☐ Romance
☐ Caring	☐ Help others	☐ Risk-taking
☐ Challenge	☐ Help society	☐ Self-expression
☐ Change	☐ Humor	☐ Spirituality
☐ Contribution	☐ Harmony	☐ Success
☐ Collaboration	☐ Honesty	☐ Service
☐ Community	☐ Joy	☐ Stability
☐ Connectedness	☐ Knowledge	☐ Time Freedom
☐ Comradeship	☐ Lack of pretense	☐ Tradition
☐ Creativity	☐ Leadership	☐ Trust
☐ Directness	☐ Leisure	☐ Vitality
☐ Economic security	☐ Lightness	☐ Wealth
☐ Empowerment	☐ Location	☐ Wisdom
☐ Excellence	☐ Loyalty	☐ Zest
☐ Excitement	☐ Nurturing	☐ Add your own _____
☐ Elegance	☐ Orderliness	
☐ Family happiness	☐ Partnership	
☐ Free spirit	☐ Participation	

PERSONAL WELL-BEING VISION™

After you and your coach have formed a trusting relationship and you have completed some assessments your coach will likely want you to create a Personal Well-Being Vision. This compelling vision of you at your best will provide you energy – it will be an attractive picture of what is most important to you that will pull you forward. Your vision will open doors for you – it will help you tap into your motivation, empower you, and help you determine if your actions are going in the right direction for you.

My Personal Well-Being Vision

Please answer the following questions to create your Personal Well-Being Vision (PWBV):

Create Your Ideal Personal Well-Being Vision Statement

After reviewing the specific goals and behaviors on which you want to focus your coaching efforts from the Well-Being Scale, imagine you're living them significantly more effectively than you are currently. Describe your ideal image of yourself with respect to these well-being practices and behaviors.

Use the lines below to write a description of your ideal personal well-being vision of yourself:

_____

_____

_____

_____

_____

_____

_____

What are the most important elements of this vision and why? _____

_____

What have been your best experiences with elements similar to this vision when you felt particularly healthy, happy and engaged? Please be specific._____

_____

_____

What values does your personal well-being vision support?_____

_____

_____

What are the good things that come from moving forward toward this ideal well-being vision? _____

_____

_____

How large is the gap between where you are now and your ideal well-being vision? _____

_____

_____

What strengths can you draw on, or what strengths can you use in a new way, that will help you move forward on your personal well-being vision? _____

_____

_____

Who and what will support you moving forward towards your ideal well-being vision? How will this support be realized/facilitated? _____

_____

_____

GOAL DESIGN

After you have completed assessments and completed your Personal Well-Being Vision you are ready to turn your vision into specific goals. Research teaches us goals work best when they are:

SPECIFIC – Specific goals help you to create behaviors that can be measured and time-lined

MEASUREABLE – Measurable goals help you determine your success

ACTION-BASED – Action-based goals tell you what to do this week

REALISTIC – Ultimately you want to achieve your goals so realistic goals are attainable

TIME-LINED – Time-lined goals add a level of concreteness to your planning which is motivating and helps you determine when you are successful and contributes to rapid progress

Specific:

What specifically do you want to accomplish? _____

_____

What will it look like when you achieve this goal? _____

_____

Measurable:

What would be a way of stating that goal so your progress toward it is measurable? _____

_____

_____

Action-Based:

What are examples of specific actions or behaviors that you will take regularly to help achieve this

goal? _____

_____

Realistic:

How much is this goal within your capabilities? _____

_____

If this goal is a significant stretch for you, how likely will you be able to succeed with this goal if you obtain significant support? _____

_____

Time-lined:

When specifically will you practice the behaviors that will help you achieve this goal? _____

_____

When will you have reached this goal or have established these behaviors as a habit? _____

_____

MY PERSONALITY TYPE

Your coach may ask you to take the Myers-Briggs Type Inventory (MBTI). There are 16 different personality types. Knowing your personality type increases your self-awareness, and that self-awareness can help you achieve your goals. Different personalities make decisions differently, recharge their batteries differently, handle information differently and manage their life differently.

Here are brief definitions of the eight terms that make up the MBTI personality type report:

How do you get energized: Do you find you focus on the outer world or on your own inner world to get more energy? This is called **Extraversion (E) or Introversion (I).**

Information: Do you prefer to focus on information you take in, for example what you hear and what you see, or do you prefer to interpret and add meaning to that information? This is called **Sensing (S) or Intuition (N).**

Decisions: When making decisions, do you prefer to first look at logical and consistent approaches, or do you focus on how people are going to feel about the decision and their special circumstances? This is called **Thinking (T) or Feeling (F).**

Lifestyle: In dealing with the outside world, do you prefer to get things decided and settled, or do you prefer to stay open to new information and options? This is called **Judging (J) or Perceiving (P).**

Your Personality Type: When you decide on your preference in each category, you have *your own personality type,* which can be expressed as a code with four letters.

The 16 personality types of the Myers-Briggs Type Indicator® instrument are listed here. Put a check mark in what your verified type is. Verified type means that after you have taken the assessment, you reflect on your results, discuss them with your coach, and then you decide what your actual type is. Usually the MBTI assessment results feel accurate to the person but sometimes you may find one letter is off, so you choose, after reflection, what your verified personalilty type is.

Please mark the box indicating what your verified type is and note if you feel it is a clear preference, a moderate preference, a slight preference or you feel you have no preference (midzone).

ISTJ	ISFJ	INFJ	INTJ

ISTP	ISFP	INFP	INTP

ESTP	ESFP	ENFP	ENTP

ESTJ	ESFJ	ENFJ	ENTJ

MY STRENGTHS

My Top 5 Strengths from the StrengthFinder are:

_____

_____

_____

_____

How well do you feel the StrengthsFinder results fit you?

_____

_____

_____

_____

My Top 5 Character Strengths from the Values in Action Inventory of Strengths (VIA-IS) are:

_____

_____

_____

_____

How well do you feel the VIA-IS results fit you?

_____

_____

_____

_____

_____

THE AUERBACH GOOD™ MODEL OF COACHING

Your coach will use a coaching model to facilitate your success in coaching. Many highly trained coaches use the Auerbach GOOD™ Coaching Model. Here is some general information on the coaching model so you understand that your coach uses a well-developed method to assist you. The four elements of the model are:

G—Goal

O—Options

O—Obstacles

D—Do

Here is an overview of the primary questions that are woven into the coaching session utilizing the Auerbach GOOD™ Model of coaching. The foundation of the coaching relationship must first be established by creating an effective coach-client relationship also known as the coaching alliance. The four principal questions of the Auerbach GOOD™ Model of Coaching, which can be asked in many different ways, are:

- What are your most important goals you want to move forward in our coaching work together?

- What options are there to move forward on these goals?

- What obstacles may get in the way and what will you do to manage them if they arise?

- Now that you've discussed your most important goals, your options, potential obstacles and how you will manage them, what specifically are you going to do and when are you going to do it?

MY ACTION COACHING PLAN

My Specific Goals	Options Brainstorm	Obstacles	Obstacle Management Plan (OMP)	The Commitments I will Make and When I Will Put them into Action	Who I Will Tell and Who Will Provide Support

OPTIONS BRAINSTORMING WORKSHEET

Identifying options is a critical step between visualizing your ideal future and turning it into reality. Working with a supportive coach enables you to think outside the box and explore multiple options that could help you accomplish your goals. Brainstorming options allows creative ideas to flourish. There are two elements to brainstorming — idea divergence (the freewheeling part) and idea convergence (the winnowing part). After you and your coach brainstorm how you can move forward you will also engage in a thought-partner dialogue to choose which are the best options for your situation.

What are at least three options of how you could move forward on this goal? _____
_____
_____

What is another option? _____
_____

What is another step you could do? _____
_____

If you went way outside the box what could you try? _____
_____
_____

What have you done in the past in similar situations? _____
_____
_____

You mentioned talking with your spouse as an option. Who else could you involve? _____
_____
_____

Since many ideas you have come up with involve doing this by yourself, what would be ways others could help? _____
_____

Which option do you want to pursue first? _____
_____

THINKING ERRORS

These are thinking errors that if left unchecked can lead to poor mood and conflict in relationships. After you learn what the major thinking errors are you can use the Constructive Thinking Plan form to adjust them.

All or Nothing Thinking

Sometimes called black and white thinking.

Example: "If I don't do it perfectly, I failed."

Over- generalizing

"everything is always rubbish"

"nothing good ever happens"

Being overly broad in the conclusions drawn.

Something bad happens and the conclusion is *"nothing good ever happens".*

Mental filter

Only paying attention to certain types of evidence.

Seeing failures, but not seeing successes.

Disqualifying the positive

Discounting the good things that have happened.

Example: "That doesn't count".

Mind Reading

Imagining we know what others are thinking.

Fortune Telling: *Thinking we can predict the future.*

Catastrophizing and Minimization

Blowing things out of Proportion (catastrophizing), or inappropriately shrinking something to make it seem less important (minimization).

Emotional reasoning

Assuming that because we feel a certain way that it must be true.

Example: "I feel stupid so I must be an idiot."

Labeling

Assigning labels to ourselves or other people.

"I'm a loser."
"I'm completely useless."
"They're such an idiot".

MY CONSTRUCTIVE THINKING PLAN

Automatic Thought	Is it a thinking error? Yes or No	Is it a helpful thought? Yes or No	What is a more accurate and helpful thought?	What is the benefit of thinking a more accurate and constructive thought?	How I will turn a more constructive thought into an affirmation	When will I practice this affirmation?

OBSTACLE BUSTING WORKSHEET

After you have identified your well-being goals, your Personal Well-Being Vision, and your options you may move forward quickly on your goals. However, sometimes it is not that easy. Coaching clients often run into obstacles. Hence the third element of the GOOD model of coaching is exploring and mentally rehearsing how to manage obstacles that may arise.

Here are some coaching questions useful during the Obstacles stage of the
Auerbach GOOD™ Coaching Model:

What might get in your way and what will you do if that occurs? _____
_____
_____

What challenges might present themselves that could interfere with you achieving your goal?
_____
_____

How would you respond to an unexpected obstacle or challenge that got in the way of moving forward on this goal? _____
_____
_____

What might be inner obstacles that might get in the way—which originate within you?_____
_____
_____

What external challenges—that are outside of you—might there be, which could interfere with moving forward with this action? _____
_____
_____

What do you need to reach this goal? _____
_____

I've heard you say you don't have time to do this. What are three options for how you could find the time? _____
_____
_____

How could you change your behavior or timetable to make this goal achievable? _____

_____

_____

What strengths could you tap into to overcome this obstacle? _____

_____

_____

Who do you know who could help you with this? _____

_____

How have you overcome obstacles like this in similar situations?_____

_____

_____

What could you change about you to change your situation? _____

_____

_____

Let's assume for a minute this situation is somehow designed for your inner growth as a person. If that were true, what is the opportunity? _____

_____

Imagine at age 80 you are telling your story to a grandchild. What would you like to be able to tell him or her about how you responded to challenges? _____

_____

If you were the best you can be, operating at your full potential—then what would you do?

_____

_____

If you woke up with a heart full of courage, what would you do to get beyond this obstacle? _____

_____

_____

SELF-MANAGEMENT ACTION PLAN

Name_____ Date_____

Log your answers to these questions twice a day for seven days.

What am I thinking right now?_____

_____

_____

_____

What am I feeling right now? _____

_____

_____

_____

What do I want to feel or accomplish right now? _____

_____

_____

_____

Am I thinking or doing anything that might block me from feeling or accomplishing what I want? If so, what? _____

_____

_____

What are one or two steps I will do right now to get the outcome I want? _____

_____

_____

_____

COACHING LEARNING JOURNAL

As you go through the coaching process you will have many insights and experiences, as well as complete many coaching homework assignments. Please use these pages to journal in a manner that is helpful for you.

_____

_____

_____

_____

_____

_____

_____

_____

_____

_____

_____

_____

_____

_____

_____

_____

_____

_____

_____

_____

_____

_____

_____

_____